D0300729

smarties
HILARIOUSLY FUNNY VERSE

Chosen by Sandy Ransford

Illustrations by David Mostyn

Robinson Children's Books

First published in the UK by Robinson Children's Books,
an imprint of Constable & Robinson Ltd, 2000

Constable & Robinson Ltd
3 The Lanchesters
162 Fulham Palace Road
London
W6 9ER

This collection © Sandy Ransford 2000
Illustrations © David Mostyn 2000
Illustrations on pages 6, 7, 79, 131, 150 and 151
© Colin McNaughton

NESTLÉ and SMARTIES are registered trademarks of Société
des Produits Nestlé S.A. 1800 Vevey, Switzerland.
© 2000 Société des Produits Nestlé S.A. Vevey, Switzerland.
Trade Mark Owners.

All rights reserved. This book is sold subject to the condition
that it shall not, by way of trade or otherwise, be lent,
re-sold, hired out or otherwise circulated in any form of
binding or cover other than that in which it is published and
without a similar condition including this condition being
imposed on the subsequent purchaser.

A copy of the British Library Cataloguing in Publication Data
for this title is available from the British Library

ISBN 1-84119-158-2

Printed and bound in the EC

10 9 8 7 6 5 4 3 2

Contents

Introduction

Where Does Laughter Begin?

Does it start in your head
and spread to your toe?

Does it start in your cheeks
and grow downwards so
till your knees feel weak?

Does it start with a tickle
in your tummy so
till you want to jump right out

of all your skin?
Or does laughter simply begin

with your mouth?

John Agard

In this book laughter begins at the beginning and goes on right through to the end. There are poems about friends and poems about enemies; poems about school and poems about families; poems about animals, food, horrible fates – and even those things polite people don't want to talk about. Some are old favourites, some were classics when your parents were young and many are brand-new. But they all have one thing in common – they're very, very funny and guaranteeed to keep you laughing from cover to cover.

Creatures Small and Great

The Worm's Refusal

'This book's revolting!'
said the worm in a rage.
'I wouldn't be seen dead
on a single page.
I'm off. I'm leaving,
and that's that!
Wait . . . no!
don't slam it shut yet . . .
Aaaaaaargh!' SPLAT!

Tony Mitton

I wish I was

I wish I was a little grub
With whiskers round my tummy;
I'd climb into a honey-pot
And make my tummy gummy.

Anon.

A centipede was happy quite,
Until a frog in fun
Said, 'Pray, which leg comes after which?'
This raised her mind to such a pitch,
She lay distracted in a ditch
Considering how to run.

Anon.

The Termite

Some primal termite knocked on wood
And tasted it and found it good,
And that is why your cousin May
Fell through the parlour floor today.

Ogden Nash

The Crocodile With Toothache

In all my life (I'm eighty-four!),
  The saddest thing I ever saw
Was in the swamps of Uskabore –
  The crocodile with toothache.

He whined and wailed, he bit his fist.
  He called for an anaesthetist.
  But tell me, how does one assist
  The crocodile with toothache?

When they heard the awful sound,
  The people came from miles around
And on the river bank they found
  The crocodile with toothache!

Then, from the people standing there,
 Emerged a hero, bold and fair.
He said: 'Stand back and I'll repair
 The crocodile with toothache!'

The hero bold said: 'Open wide!'
 The crocodile looked up and smiled
And said: 'Why don't you come inside
 The crocodile with toothache!'

He swallowed GULP! to our disgust,
 And swam off laughing, fit to bust,
The lesson here is never trust
 The crocodile with toothache!

Colin McNaughton

Quick, Quick, the Cat's Been Sick

Quick, quick,
The cat's been sick.

Where? Where?
Under the chair.

Hasten, hasten,
Fetch the basin.

No, no,
Fetch the po.

Kate, Kate, you're far too late,
The carpet's in a dreadful state.

Children's playground song

Rhinoceroses

No one for spelling at a loss is
Who boldly spells rhinocerosses;
I've known a few (I can't say lots)
Who call the beasts rhinocerots,
Though they are not so bad, say I,
As those who say rhinoceri,
One I have heard (O holy Moses!)
Who plainly said rhinoceroses,
Another one – a brilliant boy –
Insists that it's rhinoceroi –
The moral that I'll draw from these is
The plural's what one darn well pleases.

Anon.

Orion

Orion was a witches' cat.
He'd been employed for ages
by Sybil, quite the meanest witch,
who paid him measly wages.

She'd put the evil eye on him.
He'd tremble in his boots.
She fed him slimy tadpole stews
with dandelion roots.

And, when he howled in protest
she'd get him by the ear
and send him into orbit
with a kick right up the rear.

One day her loo refused to flush.
Orion was in pain.
She used him as a toilet brush.
He'd water on the brain.

It's said that moggies have nine lives.
Orion, he'd had eight!
He'd hand his resignation in
before it was too late.

His spirit rose, a wizard thought
came to him from the gloom.
He'd cast a really purrfect spell
on Sybil's flying broom.

He said '*Farewell you horrid hag.*'
She lunged at him and missed.
Her corsets ended up in knots,
her knickers in a twist.

She took off at the witching hour
and cursed her absent cat.
Her broomstick started stalling 'cos
the batteries were flat.

The sea was shining far below.
Before she'd time to think,
she'd done a double somersault
and landed in the drink.

Orion got another job
and now he's safe from harm.
He's working for a magic witch
and lapping up her charm.

Lydia Robb

Ode to an Extinct Dinosaur

Iguanadon, I loved you,
With all your spiky scales,
Your massive jaws,
Impressive claws
And teeth like horseshoe nails.

Iguanadon, I loved you.
It moved me close to tears
When first I read
That you've been dead
For ninety million years.

Doug MacLeod

Down the Stream the Swans All Glide

Down the stream the swans all glide;
It's quite the cheapest way to ride.
Their legs get wet,
Their tummies wetter:
I think after all
The bus is better.

Spike Milligan

Milly

Milly was a game old bird
Although she was a cow.
She wanted to be famous
But didn't know quite how.

For she was weary munching grass
And cheesed off chewing cud.
'Stuck in a field's no joke,' she said,
'Up to your ears in mud.'

One day she had a bright idea.
A brainwave, so she thought.
She'd get herself the proper gear
And be an astronaut.

Now Milly didn't beef about.
She made her tail a rudder.
She glued antennae to one horn,
A compass to her udder.

Then Milly took a flying leap.
She aimed for planet Mars.
Her hoof caught in a conifer
And all she saw was stars.

She never walked the Milky Way
Hoof-loose and fancy free.
She's stuck just like a fairy cow
Upon the Christmas tree.

                              Lydia Robb

Emus

To amuse
   emus
on warm summer nights.

   Kiwis
do wiwis
from spectacular heights.

Roger McGough

The Truth about the Abominable Footprint

The Yeti's a Beast
Who lives in the East
    And suffers a lot from B.O.
His hot hairy feet
Stink out the street
    So he cools them off in the snow.

Michael Baldwin

The Rabbit's Christmas Carol

I'm sick as a parrot,
I've lost me carrot,
I couldn't care less if it's
Christmas Day.

I'm sick as a parrot,
I've lost me carrot,
So get us a lettuce
Or . . . go away!

Kit Wright

A Day in the Life of Danny the Cat

Danny wakes up
Eats
Finds a private place in the garden,
He returns
Plays with the plants
And sleeps.

Danny wakes up
Eats
Inspects the garden
Finds a cosy place
And sleeps.

Danny wakes up
Comes indoors
Inspects the carpet
Scratches himself
And sleeps.

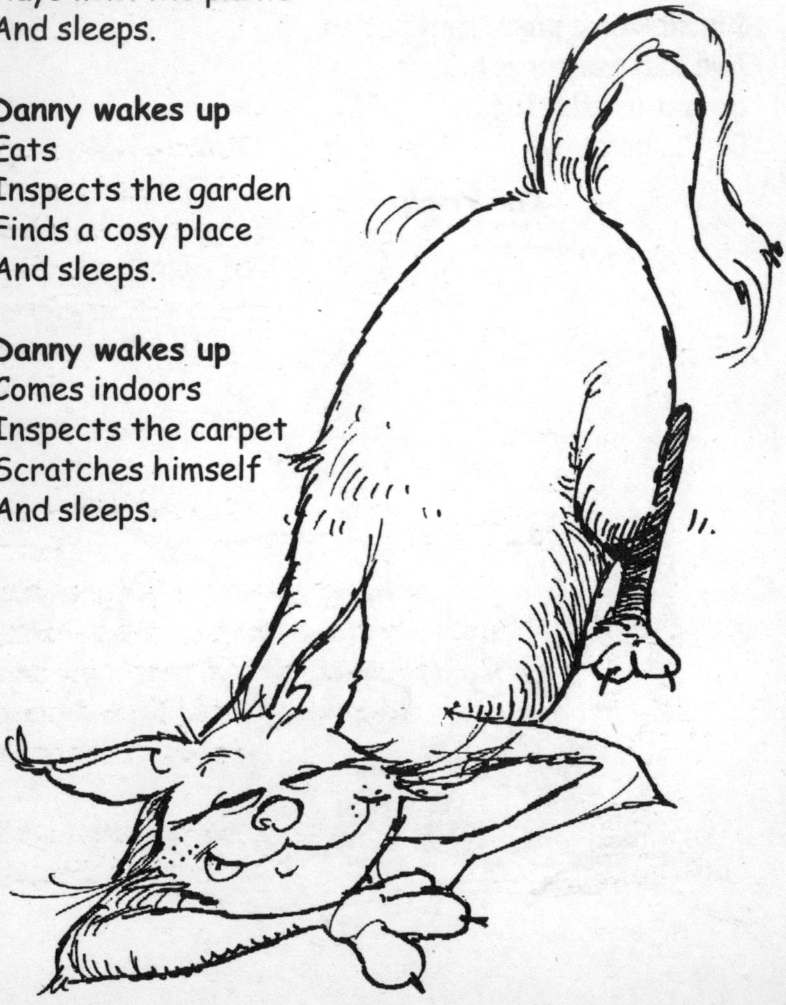

Danny wakes up
Goes in the garden
Over the fence
Has a fight with Ginger
Makes a date with Sandy
Climbs on to next door's shed
And sleeps.

Danny wakes up
Comes indoors
Rubs up the chair leg
Rubs up a human leg
Sharpens his claws
On a human leg
Eats
And sleeps.

Danny wakes up
Eats
Watches a nature programme
Finds a private place in the garden,
Finds Sandy in next door's garden
Next door's dog finds Danny
Sandy runs north

Danny runs home
Eats an sleeps.

Danny wakes up
Checks for mice
Checks for birds
Checks for dogs
Checks for food
Finds a private place in the garden
Eats
And sleeps.

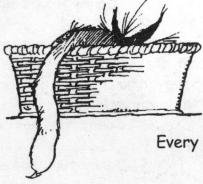

Danny has hobbies,
Being stroked
Car watching
And smelling feet
He loves life,
Keeps fit
And keeps clean,
Every night he covers himself
In spit,
Then he eats
And sleeps.

Benjamin Zephaniah

Camel

Shape lumpy,
Back humpy,
Legs clumpy,
Feet stumpy,
Ride bumpy,
Mood grumpy.

Tim Hopkins

Family
Freak-out

You are old, Father William

'You are old, Father William,' the young man said,
   'And your hair has become very white;
And yet you incessantly stand on your head –
   Do you think, at your age, it is right?'

'In my youth,' Father William replied to his son,
   'I feared it might injure the brain;
But, now that I'm perfectly sure I have none,
   Why, I do it again and again.'

'You are old,' said the youth, 'as I mentioned
     before,
   And have grown most uncommonly fat;
Yet you turned a back-somersault in at the door –
   Pray, what is the reason of that?'

'In my youth,' said the sage, as he shook his grey
     locks,
   'I kept all my limbs very supple
By the use of this ointment – one shilling the box –
   Allow me to sell you a couple.'

'You are old,' said the youth, 'and your jaws are too
     weak
   For anything tougher than suet;
Yet you finished the goose, with the bones and the
     beak –
   Pray, how did you manage to do it?'

'In my youth,' said his father, 'I took to the law,
    And argued each case with my wife;
And the muscular strength which it gave to my jaw
    Has lasted the rest of my life.'

'You are old,' said the youth, 'one would hardly
        suppose
    That your eye was as steady as ever;
Yet you balanced an eel on the end of your nose –
    What made you so awfully clever?'

'I have answered three questions, and that is
        enough,'
    Said his father; 'don't give yourself airs!
Do you think I can listen all day to such stuff?
    Be off, or I'll kick you downstairs!'

Lewis Carroll

Memory Lane

Whenever I go to my Gran's for tea
She tells amazing tales to me.

Like:
When she was only 9 years old,
She invented a cure for the common cold.

When she was only 17,
She starred in a film called *The African Queen*.

When she was only 24,
She married a Sultan from Singapore.

When she was only 39,
She commanded a sub and disabled a mine.

When she was only 53,
She forecast the weather on breakfast TV.

When she was only 75,
She tackled a tiger that ate her alive.

When she was only 87,
She remembered her trip on Apollo 11.

My Mum says my Gran
Spent her lifetime in Staines,
And married a man
With a passion for drains,

And she's never been further
Than Chessington Zoo.
But I don't think *that's* true.

Do you?

Justin Scroggie

Measles in the Ark

The night it was horribly dark,
The measles broke out in the Ark;
Little Japheth, and Shem, and all the young Hams,
Were screaming at once for potatoes and clams.
And 'What shall I do,' said poor Mrs Noah,
'All alone by myself in this terrible shower?
I know what I'll do: I'll step down in the hold,
And wake up a lioness grim and old,
And tie her close to the children's door,
And give her a ginger-cake to roar
At the top of her voice for an hour or more;
And I'll tell the children to cease their din,
Or I'll let that grim old party in,
To stop their squeazles and likewise their measles.'
She practised this with the greatest success:
She was everyone's grandmother, I guess.

Susan Coolidge

Daddy Fell into the Pond

Everyone grumbled. The sky was grey.
We had nothing to do and nothing to say.
We were nearing the end of a dismal day.
And there seemed to be nothing beyond,
   Then
      Daddy fell into the pond!

And everyone's face grew merry and bright,
And Timothy danced for sheer delight.
'Give me the camera, quick, oh quick!
He's crawling out of the duckweed!' Click!

Then the gardener suddenly slapped his knee,
And doubled up, shaking silently,
And the ducks all quacked as if they were daft,
And it sounded as if the old drake laughed.
Oh, there wasn't a thing that didn't respond
   When
      Daddy fell into the pond!

Alfred Noyes

My Dad, Your Dad

My dad's fatter than your dad,
Yes, my dad's fatter than yours:
If he eats any more he won't fit in the house,
He'll have to live out of doors.

Yes, but my dad's balder than your dad,
My dad's balder, OK,
He's only got two hairs left on his head
And both are turning grey.

Ah, but my dad's thicker than your dad,
My dad's thicker, all right.
He has to look at his watch to see
If it's noon or the middle of the night.

Yes, but my dad's more boring than your dad.
If he ever starts counting sheep
When he can't get to sleep at night, he finds
It's the sheep that go to sleep.

But my dad doesn't mind your dad.
Mine quite likes yours too.
I suppose they don't always think much of US!
That's true, I suppose, that's true.

Kit Wright

Questions, Quistions and Quoshtions

Daddy how does an elephant feel
When he swallows a piece of steel?
Does he get drunk
And fall on his trunk
Or roll down the road like a wheel?

Daddy what would a pelican do
If he swallowed a bottle of glue?
Would his beak get stuck
Would he run out of luck
And lose his job at the zoo?

Son tell me tell me true,
If I belted you with a shoe,
Would you fall down dead?
Would you go up to bed?
– Either of those would do.

Spike Milligan

Night Starvation or The Biter Bit

At night my Uncle Rufus
(Or so I've heard it said)
Would put his teeth into a glass
Of water by his bed.

At three o'clock one morning
He woke up with a cough,
And as he reached out for his teeth –
They bit his hand right off.

Carey Blyton

Auntie, did you feel no pain
Falling from that apple tree?
Will you do it, please, again?
'Cos my friend here didn't see.

Harry Graham

My Sister Laura

My sister Laura's bigger than me
And lifts me up quite easily.
I can't lift her, I've tried and tried;
She must have something heavy inside.

Spike Milligan

Susie had a Baby

Susie had a baby
She called him Tiny Tim
She put him in the bathtub
To see if he could swim
He drank up all the water
He ate up all the soap
He tried to eat the bathtub
But it wouldn't go down his throat.
Susie called the doctor
Susie called the nurse
Susie called the lady with the alligator purse.
Mumps said the doctor
Measles said the nurse
Chickenpox said the lady with the alligator purse.
Out went the doctor
Out went the nurse
Out went the lady with the alligator purse.

Traditional rhyme

Those We Love?

Back Chat

Are you the guy
That told the guy
That I'm the guy
Who gave the guy
The black eye?
No, I'm not the guy
Who told the guy
That you're the guy
Who gave the guy
The black eye.

Traditional

I Hate Harry

I hate Harry like . . . like . . . OOO!
I hate Harry like . . . GEE!
I hate that Harry like – poison.
I hate! hate! hate! HAR-RY!

Rat! Dope! Skunk! Bum! Liar!
Dumber than the dumbest dumb flea!
BOY! . . . do I hate Harry,
I hate him the most that can be.

I hate him a hundred, thousand, million
Doubled, and multiplied by three,
A skillion, trillion, zillion more times
Than Harry, that rat, hates me.

Miriam Chaikin

The rain makes all things beautiful,
The grass and flowers too.
If rain makes all things beautiful
Why doesn't it rain on you?

Anon.

Oh Honey!

Oh honey, you're a funny 'un,
With a face like a pickled onion,
A nose like a squashed tomato,
And teeth like green peas.

Children's playground rhyme

Grow Up

Grow up, grow up.
Every time I look at you
I throw up.

Children's playground rhyme

Roses Are Red

Roses are red, violets are blue,
Onions stink, and so do you.

Roses are red, cabbages are green,
My face may be funny, but yours is a scream.

Autograph verses

Happy Birthday To You!

Happy birthday to you!
Squashed tomatoes and stew;
Bread and butter in the gutter,
Happy birthday to you!

Children's playground rhyme

There She Goes

There she goes, there she goes,
Piddly heels and pointed toes,
Look at her feet,
She thinks she's neat,
Long black stockings and dirty feet.

Children's playground rhyme

A Pinch and a Punch

A pinch and a punch
For the first of the month,
And no returns.

A pinch and a kick
For being so quick.

A slap in the eye
For being so sly.

A pinch and a blow
For being so slow.

Now don't be so fast
Because I'm the last
– to punch you!

Children's playground game

Wishes of An Elderly Man

I wish I loved the Human Race;
I wish I loved its silly face;
I wish I liked the way it walks;
I wish I liked the way it talks;
And when I'm introduced to one
I wish I thought *What Jolly Fun*!

Sir Walter Raleigh

My Party

My parents said I could have a party
And that's just what I did.

Dad said, 'Who had you thought of inviting?'
I told him. He said, 'Well, you'd better start writing,'
And that's just what I did.

To:
Phyllis Willis, Horace Morris,
Nancy, Clancy, Bert and Gert Sturt,
Dick and Mick and Nick Crick.
Ron, Don, John,
Dolly, Molly, Polly –
Neil Peel –
And my dear old friend, Dave Dirt.

I wrote, 'Come along, I'm having a party.'
And that's just what they did.

They all arrived with huge appetites
As Dad and I were fixing the lights.
I said, 'Help yourself to the drinks and bites!'
And that's just what they did.
All of them:

Phyllis Willis, Horace Morris,
Nancy, Clancy, Bert and Gert Sturt,
Dick and Mick and Nick Crick.
Ron, Don, John,
Dolly, Molly, Polly –
Neil Peel –
And my dear old friend, Dave Dirt.

Now, I had a good time and as far as I could tell,
The party seemed to go pretty well –
Yes, that's just what it did.

Then Dad said, 'Come on, just for fun,
Let's have a *turn* from everyone!'
And a turn's just what they did.
All of them:

Phyllis Willis, Horace Morris,
Nancy, Clancy, Bert and Gert Sturt,
Dick and Mick and Nick Crick,
Ron, Don, John,
Dolly, Molly, Polly –
Neil Peel
And my dear old friend, Dave Dirt.

AND THIS IS WHAT THEY DID:

Phyllis and Clancy
And Horace and Nancy
Did a song and dance number
That was really fancy –

Dolly, Molly, Polly,
Ron, Don and John
Performed a play
That went on and on and on –

Gert and Bert Sturt,
Sister and brother,
Did an imitation of
Each other.
(Gert Sturt put on Bert Sturt's shirt
And Bert Sturt put on Gert Sturt's skirt.)

Neil Peel
All on his own
Danced an eightsome reel.

Dick and Mick
And Nicholas Crick
Did a most *ingenious*
Conjuring trick.

And my dear old friend, Dave Dirt,
Was terribly sick
All over the flowers.
We cleaned it up.
It took *hours*.

But as Dad said, giving a party's not easy.
You really
Have to
Stick at it.
I agree. And if Dave gives a party
I'm certainly
Going to be
Sick at it.

Kit Wright

An Evening in November

'Twas an evening in November,
    As I very well remember,
I was strolling down the street in drunken pride,
    But my knees were all a-flutter,
    So I landed in the gutter,
And a pig came up and lay down by my side.

    Yes, I lay there in the gutter,
    Thinking thoughts I could not utter,
When a colleen passing by did softly say:
    'Ye can tell a man that boozes
    By the company he chooses.'
At that the pig got up and walked away.

                                    Anon.

School
Daze

The ABC

'Twas midnight in the schoolroom
And every desk was shut,
When suddenly from the alphabet
Was heard a loud 'Tut-tut!'

Said A to B, 'I don't like C;
His manners are a lack.
For all I ever see of C
Is a semicircular back!'

'I disagree,' said D to B,
'I've never found C so.
From where *I* stand, he seems to be
An uncompleted O.'

C was vexed. 'I'm much perplexed,
You criticise my shape.
I'm made like that, to help spell Cat
And Cow and Cool and Cape.'

'He's right,' said E; said F, 'Whoopee!'
Said G, ''Ip, 'Ip, 'ooray!'
'You're dropping me,' roared H to G.
'Don't do it please, I pray!'

'Out of my way,' LL said to K.
'I'll make poor I look ill.'
To stop this stunt, J stood in front,
And presto! ILL was JILL.

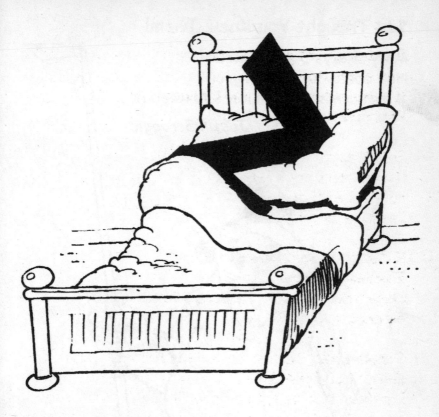

'U know,' said V, 'that W
Is twice the age of me,
For as a Roman V is five
I'm half as young as he.'

X and Y yawned sleepily,
'Look at the time!' they said.
They all jumped in to beddy byes
And the last one in was Z!

Spike Milligan

You Thought You Knew Them!

Mary, Mary, Quite Contrary,
How does your garden grow?
A man comes twice a week to weed it.

Justin Scroggie

Mary had a little lamb –
You've heard this tale before.
But did you know she passed her plate
And had a little more?

Anon.

Fighting Clocks

Hickory, dickory, dock,
Two mice ran up the clock.
The clock struck one –
But the other one got away.

Anon.

Pat-a-Cake, Pat-a-Cake

Pat-a-Cake, Pat-a-Cake,
Baker's Man,
I'd change your name as fast as you can.

Justin Scroggie

The Real Meaning

Twinkle, twinkle, little star,
I don't wonder what you are:
You're the cooling down of gases
Forming into solid masses.

Anon.

Baa, Baa, Black Sheep

Baa, Baa, Black Sheep,
Have you any wool?
What d'you think I'm wearing – an anorak?

Justin Scroggie

Dirty Socks

While shepherds washed their socks by night
All seated round the tub,
A bar of soap came tumbling down
And they began to scrub.

Anon.

Good King Wenceslas looked out
   On the Feast of Stephen;
A snowball hit him on the snout
   And made it all uneven.
Brightly shone his conk that night
   Though the pain was cruel,
Till the doctor came in sight
   Riding on a mu-oo-el.

Anon.

The Owl and the Pussy Cat

The Owl and the Pussy Cat went to sea
In a beautiful pea-green boat.
*Moral: never share a boat with someone
who thinks you're the packed-lunch.*

Justin Scroggie

The Scatterbrain

'Lost your pencil? Lost your book?
Lost your dinner money?
Soon you'll lose your head, my lad –
That will *not* be funny!'

Ronnie didn't hear a word
The angry teacher said,
His ears weren't in the classroom,
But where he'd left his head.

Tim Hopkins

I Love to do My Homework

I love to do my homework,
  it makes me feel so good,
I love to do exactly as the teacher
  says I should.
I love to do my schoolwork,
  I love it ev'ry day,
And I also love these men in white
  who are taking me away.

Traditional

Rasta Gargie

Rasta Gargie, bulla an pear,
Kiss de gals an meck dem swear;
Wen de bwoy dem come out fe play,
Rasta Gargie haul im body away.

Traditional

A humourless teacher called Hills,
Cured insomnia without using pills;
His words, dull and boring,
Led quickly to snoring,
For such were his medical skills.

Tim Hopkins

Banananananananana

I thought I'd win the spelling bee
   And get right to the top,
But I started to spell 'banana',
   And I didn't know when to stop.

William Cole

Punctuation Puzzle

Caesar entered on his head
A helmet on each foot
A sandal in his hand he had
His trusty sword to boot.

Anon.

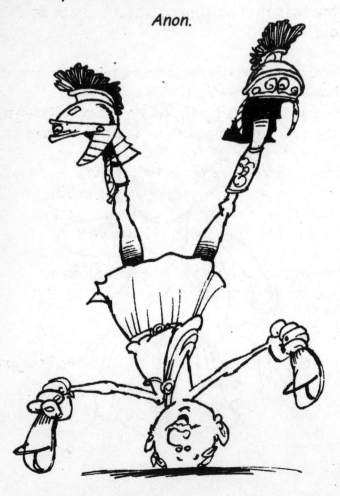

The Truth About Henry

We have a secret, the hamster and me,
The hamster who lives in a cage in 3B.
Oh it's not that I feed him my lunch through the
    bars,
Nor the fact that he ate my school project on
    Mars.

We have a secret, the hamster and me,
The hamster called Henry we keep in 3B.
Oh it's not that I smuggled him home in half-term,
Nor the fact that he picked up a terrible germ.

We have a secret, the hamster and me,
The little brown creature that sleeps in 3B.
And it's not even just that Henree is . . . a she.
It's simply that Henry went missing on me.

So the hamster so loved by the kids of 3B
I bought at a pet shop for 25p.

Yesterday.

Justin Scroggie

There's a Frog Down the Back of the Toilet, Miss

PUPIL: There's a frog down the back of the
                toilet, Miss,
            It's lodged itself under the pipe,
            And I need to go sort of desperate, Miss,
            Do you think it is likely to bite?

TEACHER: The caretaker knows of the problem,
            He's got it in hand, never fear;
            Just go to the toilet, and quickly,
            Now don't hold the lesson up, dear!

PUPIL: There's a spider on the lampshade above,
                Miss,
            And it stares when you sit on the seat,
            And I'm kind of scared it might fall, Miss,
            And I don't mean on to my feet!

TEACHER: I'm sure there is no need to worry,
             Spiders are harmless and small,
             I think an attack is unlikely,
             Go now child, or don't go at all!

PUPIL: But there's a wasp flying round the
                cistern, Miss,
            It's buzzing about to and fro,
            And I'd sort of feel quite exposed, Miss,
            Just sitting in wait down below.

TEACHER: I have no more time for your stories,
But I see that you've started to dance
From one leg on to the other,
So go now, this is your last chance!

HALF AN HOUR LATER

TEACHER: What took you so long in the toilet,
child?
You've missed half an hour of science.
Your excuse had better convince me
Or I'll punish your blatant defiance!

PUPIL: Well, while I sat on the toilet, Miss,
The wasp got caught in the web
The spider had spun just above, Miss,
It was almost touching my head!

So I grabbed up my trousers quite
smartish, Miss,
And got ready to leave pretty quick,
When I noticed my trousers were
croaking, Miss,
And I started to feel sort of sick.

And as I stood still in the corner, Miss,
My trousers were leaping about,
And I was too frightened to move, Miss,
Too frightened even to shout!

Then out of the top of my trousers, Miss,
A little frog struggled and jumped
Up to the spider and wasp, Miss,
He swallowed them both in one lump.

Then SPLASH! the frog landed in water,
Miss,
He swam around having great fun,
With legs hanging out of his mouth, Miss,
It was just like *Wildlife on One*!

Then I flushed him away down the loo,
    Miss,
He swam with the flow, without pain,
I expect he'll escape very quickly,
    Miss,
When he comes to the end of the
    drain.

TEACHER: Your tale is less than convincing,
You'll stay in at lunch for a week;
And unless you can tell me the truth,
    dear,
Please just don't bother to speak!

ENTER CARETAKER

CARETAKER: The boys' toilets are out of order,
I hope no one's playing a joke,
There's some kind of blockage to sort
    out,
A blockage that happens to croak!

Coral Rumble

We Break Up, We Break Down

We break up, we break down,
We don't care if the school falls down.
This time next week where shall we be?
Out of the gates of misery!
No more Latin, no more French,
No more sitting on the hard old bench.
No more cabbages filled with slugs,
No more drinking out of dirty old mugs.
No more spiders in my tea,
Making googly eyes at me.
Kick up tables, kick up chairs,
Kick old teacher down the stairs,
If that does not serve her right,
Blow her up with dynamite.

Anon.

Foul
Food

Little Miss Muffet

Little Miss Muffet sat on her tuffet
Eating her curds and whey.
When along came a spider
Who sat down beside her
And said, 'Too much cholesterol, I'd say.'

Anon.

Cockroach Sandwich

Cockroach sandwich
For my lunch,
Hate the taste
But love the crunch!

Colin McNaughton

I'm Going to the Garden to Eat Worms

Nobody likes me, everybody hates me,
I'm going to the garden to eat worms.
Long, thin, slimy ones, short, fat fuzzy ones,
Gooey, gooey, gooey, gooey worms.

The long, thin, slimy ones slip down easily,
The short, fat, fuzzy ones stick,
Nobody likes me, everybody hates me,
I'm going to the garden to be sick.

You cut off the heads, and suck out the juice,
And throw the skins away.
Nobody knows how I survive
On a hundred worms a day.

Anon.

Deedle, Deedle Dumpling, My Son John

Deedle, deedle dumpling, my son John,
Ate a pasty five feet long;
He bit it once, he bit it twice,
Oh, my goodness, it was full of mice!

Anon.

On Nevski Bridge

On Nevski Bridge a Russian stood,
Chewing his beard for lack of food.
Said he, 'It's tough, this stuff, to eat
But a darned sight better than shredded wheat!'

Anon.

Mister Kelly

Old Mister Kelly
Had a pimple on his belly.
His wife cut it off
And it tasted just like jelly.

Anon.

Mary Ate Jam

Mary ate jam,
Mary ate jelly,
Mary went home
With a pain in her –
Now don't get excited
Don't be misled
Mary went home
With a pain in her head.

Anon.

Henry Sutton

Henry Sutton
Made his wife
Serve him mutton
All his life.

When going to sleep,
His mind was rested
By counting the sheep
That he'd digested!

Anon.

The Epicure at Crewe

An epicure, dining at Crewe,
Found quite a large mouse in his stew;
    Said the waiter: Don't shout
    And wave it about,
Or the rest will be wanting one, too!

Anon.

Grannie Caught a Flea

ABC
My Grannie caught a flea
She salted it, and peppered it,
And had it for her tea.

Anon.

An Old Man From Peru

There was an old man from Peru
Who dreamt he was eating his shoe.
   He awoke in the night
   In a terrible fright
And found it was perfectly true.

Anon.

A lady from Louth with a lisp
Liked her sausages specially crisp.
But in trying to say
That she liked them that way
She covered her friends in a mitht.

Michael Palin

School Dinners I

What's for dinner? What's for dinner?
Irish spew, Irish spew,
Sloppy semolina, sloppy semolina,
No thank you, no thank you.

Splishy splashy custard, dead dogs' eyes,
All mixed up with giblet pies,
Spread it on the butty nice and thick,
Swallow it down with a bucket of sick.

Hotch scotch, bogie pie,
Mix it up with a dead man's eye
Hard-boiled snails, slapped on thick,
Wash it down with a cup of cold sick.

Anon.

School Dinners II

School dinners, school dinners,
Burnt baked beans, burnt baked beans,
Sloppy semolina, sloppy semolina,
I feel sick,
Get a bucket quick.

Anon.

Telly-pie-tit

Telly-pie-tit
Sat upon a wall
Eating raw cabbages,
Slugs, snails and all.

Chidren's playground rhyme

The Sausage

The sausage is a cunning bird
With feathers long and wavy;
It swims about the frying pan
And makes its nest in gravy.

Anon.

Beans

Beans, beans, good for the heart,
The more you eat, the more you fart,
The more you fart, the better you feel,
So let's have beans for every meal.

Anon.

Apple Pie

There was a young lad of St Just
Who ate apple pie till he bust;
   It wasn't the fru-it
   That caused him to do it,
What finished him off was the crust.

Anon.

Apples

Apple crumble makes you rumble,
Apple tart makes you fart,
Apple snow makes you go,
Apple bun makes you run,
Apple pie makes you sigh,
Apple cake makes you ache.

Anon.

'Waiter! This soup has a smell
Reminiscent of brimstone from hell.
    The taste is as foul
    As a decomposed owl,
And it looks like the slime on a well.'

Anon.

The Boy Stood in the Supper-room

The boy stood in the supper-room
  Whence all but he had fled;
He'd eaten seven pots of jam
  And he was gorged with bread.

'Oh, one more crust before I bust!'
  He cried in accents wild;
He licked the plates, he sucked the spoons –
  He was a vulgar child.

There came a burst of thunder-sound –
  The boy – oh! where was he?
Ask of the maid who mopped him up,
  The breadcrumbs and the tea!

Anon.

Susie

Overeating was Susie's disgrace,
She'd an appetite vulgar and base,
And the food that she gobbled
Soon afterwards wobbled
At the opposite end from her face.

Tim Hopkins

Greedy Jane

'Pudding *and* pie,'
Said Jane; 'O my!'
'Which would you rather?'
Said her father.
'Both,' cried Jane,
Quite bold and plain.

Anon.

Peas

I eat my peas with honey,
I've done it all my life.
It makes the peas taste funny,
But it keeps them on the knife.

Anon.

Bitter Butter

Betty Botter bought some butter,
But, she said, this butter's bitter;
If I put it in my batter,
It will make my batter bitter,
But a bit of better butter
Will make my batter better.
So she bought a bit of butter
Better than her bitter butter,
And she put it in her batter,
And it made her batter better,
So 'twas better Betty Botter
Bought a bit of better butter.

Anon.

Getting
Personal

My Nose

It doesn't breathe; it doesn't smell;
It doesn't feel so very well.
I am disgusted with my nose.
The only thing it does is blows.

Anon.

Do Your Ears Hang Low?

Do your ears hang low?
Do they wobble to and fro?
Can you tie them in a knot?
Can you tie them in a bow?
Can you throw them over your shoulder
Like a regimental soldier?
Do your ears hang low?

Do your ears hang high?
Do they wave up in the sky?
Do they crinkle when they're wet?
Do they straighten when they're dry?
Can you wave them at your neighbour
With a minimum of labour?
Do your ears hang high?

Traditional

True Love

Your teeth are like the stars,' he said,
And pressed her hand so white.
He spoke the truth, for, like the stars,
Her teeth came out at night.

Anon.

Teeth

English Teeth, English Teeth!
Shining in the sun
A part of British heritage
Aye, each and every one.

English Teeth, Happy Teeth!
Always having fun
Clamping down on bits of fish
And sausages half done.

English Teeth! HEROES' Teeth!
Hear them click! and clack!
Let's sing a song of praise to them –
Three Cheers for the Brown, Grey and Black.

Spike Milligan

Smelly

Here I sit all alone in the moonlight,
Abandoned by women and men,
Muttering, over and over,
'I'll never eat garlic again!'

Anon.

My Feet

The feet I wish were beautiful,
In every way are wrong:
They're skinny, white and bony,
And worst of all they pong.

Tim Hopkins

Black Socks

Black socks, they never get dirty,
The longer you wear them the stronger they get.
Sometimes I think I should wash them,
But something inside me keeps saying,
'Not yet, not yet, not yet, not yet, not yet.'

Traditional

Trainers

There's something alive in my trainers,
It lives at the toe-end,
My Mum says it's disgusting
But it cheers me up no end!

Justin Scroggie

Sam, Sam

Sam, Sam, the dirty man,
Washed his face in a frying pan;
He combed his hair with a donkey's tail,
And scratched his belly with a big toenail.

Children's playground rhyme

Papa Moses Killed a Skunk

Papa Moses killed a skunk
Mama Moses cooked the skunk
Baby Moses ate the skunk
My oh my oh how they stunk.

   Traditional American rhyme

A Riddle

Because I am by nature blind,
I wisely choose to walk behind;
However, to avoid disgrace,
I let no creature see my face.
My words are few, but spoke with sense:
And yet my speaking gives offence:
Or, if to whisper I presume,
The company will fly the room.
By all the world I am oppressed,
But my oppression gives them rest.

Jonathan Swift

Answer: A bottom

A Student from Sparta

A musical student from Sparta
Was a truly magnificent farter;
On the strength of one bean
He'd fart 'God Save The Queen',
And Beethoven's *Moonlight Sonata*.

Anon.

Under the Apple Tree

As I sat under the apple tree,
A birdie sent his love to me,
And as I wiped it from my eye,
I said, 'Thank goodness, cows can't fly.'

Anon.

The Black Cat and the White Cat

Oh! the black cat piddled in the white cat's eye,
The white cat said, 'Cor blimey!'
'I'm sorry, sir, I piddled in your eye,
I didn't know you was behind me.'

Anon.

Iced Ink

The Punk Skunk's Song

Sing a punk skunk's song:
if you like to pong;
if you like to whiff;
if you like to stink,
after me, shout out 'Iced ink!'

Try it twice a week,
if you like to reek
like a goat or polecat,
maybe a mink;
after me, shout out 'Iced ink!'

If there's dust or dirt
clinging to your shirt,
if your underwear
should be in the sink,
after me, shout out 'Iced ink!'

If you never clench
your nose at the stench,
when your nostril shocks
make the vicar blink,
after me, shout out 'Iced ink!'

If foul odour wafts
from your unwashed socks;
if your noxious feet
tend to tarnish zinc,
after me, shout out 'Iced ink!'

Sing a punk skunk's song:
if you like to pong;
if you like to whiff;
if you like to stink,
after me, shout out 'Iced ink!'

Mike Johnson

Baby on the Po

Eeny, meeny, miney, mo,
Sit the baby on the po,
When he's done,
Wipe his bum,
Tell his mummy what he's done.

Children's playground rhyme

Funny
People

You Remind Me of a Man

You remind me of a man
What man?
A man of power.
What power?
The power of hoodoo.
Who do?
You do.
Do what?
Remind me of a man.
What man?
A man of power.
What power?
The power of hoodoo.
Who do?
You do.
Do what?
Remind me of a man.
What man?
A man of . . .

Traditional

Esau

I saw Esau sawing wood,
  And Esau saw I saw him;
Though Esau saw I saw him saw
  Still Esau went on sawing.

Anon.

A Trip to Morrow

I started on a journey just about a week ago
For the little town of Morrow in the State of Ohio.
I never was a traveller and I really didn't know
That Morrow had been ridiculed a century or so.
To Morrow, to Morrow, I have to go to Morrow,
The ticket collector told me that I have to go
    tomorrow.

I went down to the depot for my ticket and applied
For tips regarding Morrow, interviewed the
    station guide.
Said I, 'My friend, I want to go to Morrow and
    return
No later than tomorrow, for I haven't time to
    burn.'
To Morrow, to Morrow, I have to go to Morrow,
The ticket collector told me that I have to go
    tomorrow.

Said he to me, 'Now let me see, if I have heard you
    right,
You want to go to Morrow and come back tomorrow
    night,
You should have gone to Morrow yesterday and
    back today,
The train to Morrow, left at two to Morrow
    yesterday.
To Morrow, to Morrow, I have to go to Morrow,
The ticket collector told me that I have to go
    tomorrow.

For if you started yesterday to Morrow, don't you
see
You should have got to Morrow and returned today
at three.
The train that started yesterday, now understand
me right,
Today it gets to Morrow and returns tomorrow
night.'
To Morrow, to Morrow, I have to go to Morrow,
The ticket collector told me that I have to go
tomorrow.

Said I, 'I guess you know it all, but kindly let me
say,
How can I go to Morrow if I leave the town today?'
Said he, 'You cannot go to Morrow today I'll have
you know,
For that train you see just leaving is the only one
to go. So –
Tomorrow, tomorrow, you'll have to go tomorrow,
The train to Morrow just left today, you'll have to
go tomorrow.

Anon.

The Mad Gardener's Song

He thought he saw an Elephant,
    That practised on a fife:
He looked again, and found it was
    A letter from his wife.
'At length I realise,' he said,
    'The bitterness of Life!'

He thought he saw a Buffalo
    Upon the chimney-piece:
He looked again, and found it was
    His Sister's Husband's Niece.
'Unless you leave this house,' he said,
    'I'll send for the Police!'

He thought he saw a Rattlesnake
    That questioned him in Greek:
He looked again, and found it was
    The Middle of Next Week.
'The one thing I regret,' he said,
    'Is that it cannot speak!'

He thought he saw a Banker's Clerk
    Descending from the bus:
He looked again, and found it was
    A Hippopotamus:
'If this should stay to dine,' he said,
    'There won't be much for us!'

He thought he saw a Kangaroo
   That worked a coffee-mill:
He looked again, and found it was
   A Vegetable-Pill.
'Were I to swallow this,' he said,
   'I should be very ill!'

He thought he saw a Coach-and-Four
   That stood beside his bed:
He looked again, and found it was
   A Bear without a Head.
'Poor thing,' he said, 'poor silly thing!
   It's waiting to be fed!'

He thought he saw an Albatross
   That fluttered round the lamp:
He looked again, and found it was
   A Penny-Postage-Stamp.
'You'd best be getting home,' he said:
   'The nights are very damp!'

He thought he saw a Garden-Door
   That opened with a key:
He looked again, and found it was
   A Double Rule of Three:
'And all its mystery,' he said,
   'Is clear as day to me!'

He thought he saw an Argument
   That proved he was the Pope:
He looked again and found it was
   A Bar of Mottled Soap.
'A fact so dread,' he faintly said,
   'Extinguishes all hope!'

Lewis Carroll

Topsyturvey-World

If the butterfly courted the bee,
   And the owl the porcupine;
If churches were built in the sea,
   And three times one was nine:
If the pony rode his master,
   If the buttercups ate the cows,
If the cat had the dire disaster
   To be worried, sir, by the mouse;
If mamma, sir, sold the baby
   To a gipsy for half-a-crown;
If a gentleman, sir, was a lady –
   The world would be Upside-Down!
If any or all of these wonders
   Should ever come about,
I should not consider them blunders,
   For I should be Inside-Out!

William Brighty Rands

Somebody said that it Couldn't be Done

Somebody said that it couldn't be done –
But he, with a grin, replied
He'd not be the one to say it couldn't be done –
Leastways, not 'til he'd tried.
So he buckled right in, with a trace of a grin;
By golly, he went right to it.
He tackled The Thing That Couldn't Be Done
And he couldn't do it.

Anon.

Sophie Charlotte Wyatt-Wyatt

Sophie Charlotte Wyatt-Wyatt
Wouldn't eat a proper diet.
All she'd eat were snails and slugs,
(She bought them by the pint in jugs!)
She grew to twelve, then through her teens,
Not tasting fish or fowl or greens.
It hasn't done her any harm,
She's small and pretty – full of charm.
Though Sophie Charlotte I adore,
She has the odd annoying flaw:
She's very shy, stays in her shell.
She's also rather slow, as well.
And when we're walking in the park,
(At my insistence, after dark!)
Miss Wyatt-Wyatt is inclined
To leave a trail of slime behind!

Colin McNaughton

The Jumblies

I

They went to sea in a Sieve, they did,
   In a Sieve they went to sea:
In spite of all their friends could say,
On a winter's morn, on a stormy day,
   In a Sieve they went to sea!
And when the Sieve turned round and round,
And every one cried, 'You'll all be drowned!'
They called aloud, 'Our Sieve ain't big,
But we don't care a button! we don't care a fig!
  In a Sieve we'll go to sea!'
   Far and few, far and few,
    Are the lands where the Jumblies live;
    Their heads are green, and their hands are blue,
    And they went to sea in a Sieve.

II

They sailed away in a Sieve, they did,
  In a Sieve they sailed so fast,
With only a beautiful pea-green veil
Tied with a riband by way of a sail,
  To a small tobacco-pipe mast;
And every one said, who saw them go,
'O won't they be soon upset, you know!
For the sky is dark, and the voyage is long,
And happen what may, it's extremely wrong
  In a Sieve to sail so fast!'
  Far and few, far and few,
    Are the lands where the Jumblies live;
  Their heads are green, and their hands are blue,
    And they went to sea in a Sieve.

III

The water it soon came in, it did,
  The water it soon came in;
So to keep them dry, they wrapped their feet
In a pinky paper all folded neat,
  And they fastened it down with a pin.
And they passed the night in a crockery-jar,
And each of them said, 'How wise we are!
Though the sky be dark, and the voyage be long,
Yet we never can think we were rash or wrong,
  While round in our Sieve we spin!'
  Far and few, far and few,
    Are the lands where the Jumblies live;
  Their heads are green, and their hands are blue,
    And they went to sea in a Sieve.

IV

And all night long they sailed away;
   And when the sun went down,
They whistled and warbled a moony song
To the echoing sound of a coppery gong,
   In the shade of the mountains brown.
'O Timballo! How happy we are,
When we live in a Sieve and a crockery-jar,
And all night long in the moonlight pale,
We sail away with a pea-green sail,
   In the shade of the mountains brown!'
  Far and few, far and few,
   Are the lands where the Jumblies live;
   Their heads are green, and their hands are blue,
   And they went to sea in a Sieve.

V

They sailed to the Western Sea, they did,
   To a land all covered with trees,
And they bought an Owl, and a useful Cart,
And a pound of Rice, and a Cranberry Tart,
   And a hive of silvery Bees.
And they bought a Pig, and some green Jack-daws,
And a lovely Monkey with lollipop paws,
And forty bottles of Ring-Bo-Ree,
   And no end of Stilton Cheese.
  Far and few, far and few,
   Are the lands where the Jumblies live;
   Their heads are green, and their hands are blue,
   And they went to sea in a Sieve.

VI

And in twenty years they all came back
  In twenty years or more,
And every one said 'How tall they've grown!
For they've been to the Lakes, and the Torrible
    Zone,
  And the hills of the Chankly Bore;'
And they drank their health, and gave them a
    feast
Of dumplings made of beautiful yeast;
And every one said, 'If we only live,
We too will go to sea in a Sieve, –
  To the hills of the Chankly Bore!'
  Far and few, far and few,
    Are the lands where the Jumblies live;
    Their heads are green, and their hands are blue,
    And they went to sea in a Sieve.

Edward Lear

Girl in Blue

I am a girl guide dressed in blue,
These are the actions I can do –
Salute to the captain.
Curtsey to the queen,
Show my panties to the football team.

Anon.

A Curious Fellow Named Kurt

A curious fellow named Kurt
Used to climb Alpine peaks in a skirt.
He said it felt nice
In the snow and the ice,
And it kept those below more alert.

Michael Palin

The Guided Missile

The choirboy threw a well-aimed dart,
When kneeling down to pray,
It pierced the wine-filled chalice,
And the priest said, 'Let us spray.'

Tim Hopkins

Fair Play

Mirror mirror on the wall
Could you please return our ball
Our football went through your crack
You have two now
Give one back.

Benjamin Zephaniah

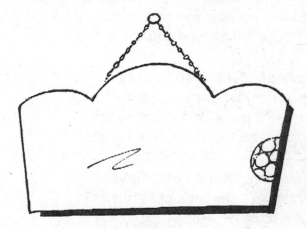

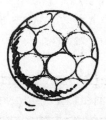

Hunter Trials

It's awf'lly bad luck on Diana,
    Her ponies have swallowed their bits;
She fished down their throats with a spanner
    And frightened them all into fits.

So now she's attempting to borrow.
    Do lend her some bits, Mummy, *do*;
I'll lend her my own for tomorrow,
    But today I'll be wanting them too.

Just look at Prunella on Guzzle,
    The wizardest pony on earth;
Why doesn't she slacken his muzzle
    And tighten the breech in his girth?

I say, Mummy, there's Mrs Geyser
    And doesn't she look pretty sick?
I bet it's because Mona Lisa
    Was hit on the hock with a brick.

Miss Blewitt says Monica threw it,
    But Monica says it was Joan,
And Joan's very thick with Miss Blewitt,
    So Monica's sulking alone.

And Margaret failed in her paces,
    Her withers got tied in a noose,
So her coronets caught in the traces
    And now all her fetlocks are loose.

Oh, it's me now. I'm terribly nervous.
    I wonder if Smudges will shy.
She's practically certain to swerve as
    Her Pelham is over one eye.

Oh wasn't it naughty of Smudges?
    Oh, Mummy, I'm sick with disgust.
She threw me in front of the Judges,
    And my silly old collarbone's bust.

John Betjeman

Little Bo Peep

Little Bo Peep
Has lost her beep
And doesn't know where to find it;
Her mobile phone
Is out on loan
With a friend she asked to mind it.

Tim Hopkins

Max Faxed the Facts

Max faxed the facts on his fax
Straight down the phone line to Mack's.
The fact Max had faxed Mack
And Mack then faxed Max back
Meant Mack faxed the facts back to Max.

Ernest Henry

Horrible Things

'What's the horriblest thing you've seen?'
Said Nell to Jean.

'Some grey-coloured, trodden-on plasticine;
On a plate, a left-over cold baked bean;
A cloak-room ticket numbered thirteen;
A slice of meat without any lean;
The smile of a spiteful fairy-tale queen;
A thing in the sea like a brown submarine;
A cheese fur-coated in brilliant green;
A bluebottle perched on a piece of sardine.
What's the horriblest thing *you've* seen?'
Said Jean to Nell.

'Your face, as you tell
Of all the horriblest things you've seen.'

Roy Fuller

Horrible
Fates

Two's Company

*The sad story of the man who didn't
believe in ghosts*

They said the house was haunted, but
He laughed at them and said, 'Tut, tut!
I've never heard such tittle-tattle
As ghosts that groan and chains that rattle;
And just to prove I'm in the right,
Please leave me here to spend the night.'

They winked absurdly, tried to smother
Their ignorant laughter, nudged each other,
And left him just as dusk was falling
With a hunchback moon and screech-owls calling.
Not that this troubled him one bit;
In fact, he was quite glad of it,
Knowing it's every sane man's mission
To contradict all superstition.

But what is that? Outside it seemed
As if chains rattled, someone screamed!
Come, come, it's merely nerves, he's certain
(But just the same, he draws the curtain).
The stroke of twelve – but there's no clock!
He shuts the door and turns the lock
(Of course, he knows that no one's there,
But no harm's done by taking care!)
Someone's outside – the silly joker,
(He may as well pick up the poker!)
That noise again! He checks the doors,
Shutters the windows, makes a pause
To seek the safest place to hide –
The cupboard's strong – he creeps inside).
'Not that there's anything to fear,'
He tells himself, when at his ear
A voice breathes softly, 'How do you do!
I am the ghost. Pray, who are you?'

Raymond Wilson

I Like to Stay Up

I like to stay up
and listen
when big people talking
jumbie stories

I does feel
so tingly and excited
inside me

But when my mother say
'Girl, time for bed'

Then is when
I does feel a dread

Then is when
I does cover up
from me feet to me head

Then is when
I does wish I didn't listen
to no stupid jumbie story

Then is when
I does wish I did read
me book instead

Grace Nichols

(Jumbie – Guyanese word for ghost)

Vampires

The vampires that bite necks in gangs,
Like a blood which is tasty and tangs,
When they've guzzled enough
Of the hot, pulsing stuff,
They say to their teeth: 'Thank you, fangs!'

Tim Hopkins

Transylvania Dreaming (cert PG)

In the middle of the night
When you're safe in bed
And the doors are locked
And the cats are fed
And it's much too bright
And sleep won't come
And there's something wrong
And you want your mum
And you hear a noise
And you see a shape
And it looks like a bat
Or a man in a cape
And you dare not breathe
And your heart skips a beat
And you're cold as ice
From your head to your feet
And you say a prayer
And you swear to be good
And you'd run for your life
If you only could
And your eyes are wide

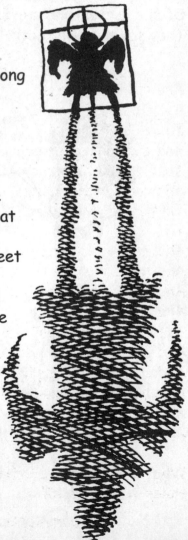

And stuck on stalks
As the thing in black
Towards you walks
And the room goes dark
And you faint clean away
And you don't wake up
Till the very next day . . .

And you open your eyes
And the sun is out
And you jump out of bed
And you sing and shout:
'It was only a dream!'
And you dance around the room
And your heart is as light
As a helium balloon
And your mum rushes in
And says: 'Hold on a sec . . .

What are those two little
Holes in your neck?'

Colin McNaughton

On the Bridge at Midnight

She stood on the bridge at midnight,
Her limbs were all a-quiver.
She gave a cough, her leg fell off,
And floated down the river.

Anon.

The Chimney Sweep

Eaver, Weaver, chimney sweeper,
    Had a wife and couldn't keep her,
Had another, didn't love her,
    Up the chimney he did shove her.

                        Anon.

Cry Baby

Cry baby, cry,
Punch him in the eye
Hang him on the lamppost
And leave him there to dry.

Anon.

Careless Willie

Willie, with a thirst for gore,
Nailed his sister to the door.
Mother said, with humour quaint:
'Now, Willie dear, don't scratch the paint.'

Anon.

There Was An Old Woman

There was an old woman who swallowed a fly,
I wonder why
She swallowed a fly.
Poor old woman, she's sure to die.

There was an old woman who swallowed a spider
That wriggled and jiggled and wriggled inside her.
She swallowed the spider to catch the fly,
I wonder why
She swallowed a fly.
Poor old woman, she's sure to die.

There was an old woman who swallowed a bird;
How absurd
To swallow a bird.
She swallowed the bird to catch the spider,
That wriggled and jiggled and wriggled inside her.
She swallowed the spider to catch the fly,
I wonder why
She swallowed a fly.
Poor old woman, she's sure to die.

There was an old woman who swallowed a cat;
Fancy that!
She swallowed a cat;
She swallowed the cat to catch the bird,
She swallowed the bird to catch the spider,
That wriggled and jiggled and wriggled inside her.

She swallowed the spider to catch the fly,
I wonder why
She swallowed a fly.
Poor old woman, she's sure to die.

There was an old woman who swallowed a dog;
Oh what a hog!
She swallowed a dog;
She swallowed the dog to catch the cat,
She swallowed the cat to catch the bird,
She swallowed the bird to catch the spider,
That wriggled and jiggled and wriggled inside her.
She swallowed the spider to catch the fly,
I wonder why
She swallowed a fly.
Poor old woman, she's sure to die.

There was an old woman who swallowed a cow;
I wonder how
She swallowed a cow;
She swallowed the cow to catch the dog,
She swallowed the dog to catch the cat;
She swallowed the cat to catch the bird,
She swallowed the bird to catch the spider,
That wriggled and jiggled and wriggled inside her.
She swallowed the spider to catch the fly,
I wonder why
She swallowed a fly.
Poor old woman, she's sure to die.

There was an old woman who swallowed a horse;
She died of course!

Anon.

Algy

Algy met a bear.
The bear met Algy.
The bear was bulgy.
The bulge was Algy.

Anon.

The Old Woman of Ryde

There was an old woman of Ryde,
Who ate some green apples and died.
The apples fermented,
Inside the lamented,
Making cider inside 'er inside.

Anon.

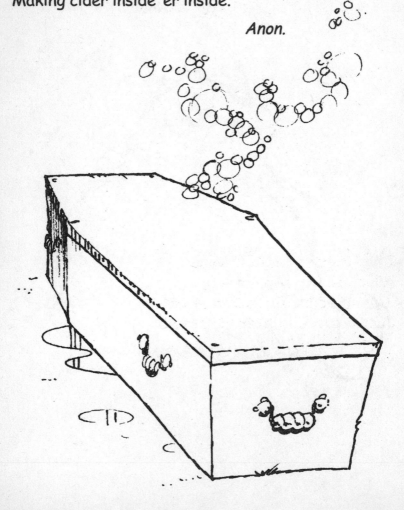

Aunt Maud

I had written to Aunt Maud
Who was on a trip abroad,
When I heard she'd died of cramp
Just too late to save the stamp.

Anon.

Notting Hill Polka

We've – had –
A Body in the house
   Since Father passed away:
He took bad on
Saturday night an' he
   Went the followin' day.

      Mum's – pulled –
      The blinds all down
         An' bought some Sherry Wine,
      An' we've put the tin
      What the Arsenic's in
         At the bottom of the
            Ser-pen-tine!

              W. Bridges-Adams

Paul

There was a young man named Paul
Who went to a fancy dress ball
He decided to risk it
And dressed up as a biscuit
But the dog ate him up in the hall.

Anon.

The Lion

Oh, weep for Mr and Mrs Bryan!
He was eaten by a lion;
Following which, the lion's lioness
Up and swallowed Bryan's Bryaness.

Ogden Nash

Grave Yard

Here lies the body
Of Tony Welch:
Exploded
With a mighty belch.

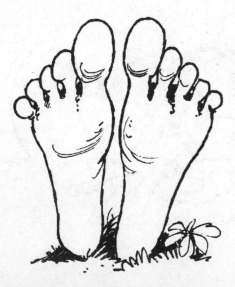

Here lies the body
Of Mary Rose
She ate the gunge
Between her toes.

Here lies the body
Of Tracey Plumb:
Sucked her body away –
– Began with her thumb!

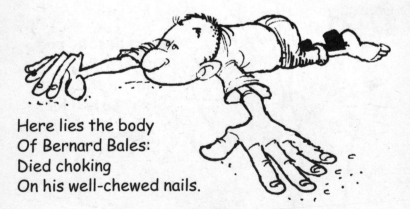

Here lies the body
Of Bernard Bales:
Died choking
On his well-chewed nails.

Here lies the body
Of Auntie Betty:
Jogged thirty miles
Drowned – far too
    sweaty.

Here lies the body
Of young Len Loader,
Gassed to death
By his body odour.

John Kitching

The End

There was an old man in a hearse
Who murmured, 'This might have been worse;
Of course, the expense,
Is simply immense,
But it doesn't come out of my purse!'

Anon.

Index of
First Lines

Acknowledgements

The author and publishers would like to thank the following people for giving permission to include in this anthology material which is their copyright. The publishers have made every effort to trace the copyright holders. If we have inadvertently omitted to acknowledge anyone we should be most grateful if this could be brought to our attention for correction at the earliest opportunity.

John Agard, c/o Caroline Sheldon Literary Agency, for 'Where Does Laughter Begin?' from *Laughter is an Egg* published by Viking Puffin 1990.

The Estate of the late John Betjeman and John Murray (Publishers) Ltd for 'Hunter Trials' by John Betjeman, from *Collected Poems*.

William Cole for 'Banananananananananana'.

Curtis Brown Ltd, London, on behalf of Grace Nichols, for 'I Like to Stay Up', © Grace Nichols 1988.

André Deutsch Ltd for 'The Termite' and 'The Lion' by Ogden Nash, from *Candy is Dandy*.

Ernest Henry for 'Max'.

Tim Hopkins for 'The Vampires that Bite Necks in Gangs', 'Camel', 'A Humourless Teacher Called Hills', 'The Scatterbrain', 'Little Bo Peep', 'My Feet', 'The Guided Missile', and 'Overeating Was Susie's Disgrace'

International Music Network for 'Night Starvation or The Biter Bit' by Carey Blyton.

Mike Johnson for 'Iced Ink'.

John Kitching for 'Grave Yard'.

Colin McNaughton and Walker Books Ltd., London, for 'Transylvania Dreaming (Cert. PG)', 'The Crocodile with Toothache', 'Cockroach Sandwich' and 'Sophie Charlotte Wyatt-Wyatt', from *Making Friends with Frankenstein* © Colin McNaughton 1993.

Spike Milligan Productions Ltd for 'Down the Stream the Swans All Glide', 'My Sister Laura', 'Teeth', 'The ABC' and 'Questions, Quistions and Quoshtions' by Spike Milligan.

Tony Mitton for 'T he Worm's Refusal'.

Penguin Books Australia Ltd for 'Ode to an Extinct Dinosaur' by Doug Macleod from *In the Garden of Bad Things*.

Penguin Books UK Ltd for 'A Day in the Life of Danny the Cat' and 'Fair Play' by Benjamin Zephaniah, from *Talking Turkeys*, and for 'The Rabbit's Christmas Carol' by Kit Wright, from *Hot Dog and Other Stories*.

Peters, Fraser & Dunlop on behalf of Roger McGough for 'Emus' by Roger McGough, © Roger McGough as printed in the original volume, and for 'Notting Hill Polka' by W. Bridges-Adams.

Random House Group Ltd. on behalf of Raymond Wilson for 'Two's Company', from *The Beaver Book of Funny Verse*, now published by Red Fox.

Random House Group Ltd. on behalf of Michael Palin for 'A Curious Fellow Named Kurt' and 'A Lady from Louth with a Lisp', from *Limericks*, published by Red Fox.

Lydia Robb for 'Orion' and 'Milly'.

Coral Rumble for 'There's a Frog Down the Back of the Toilet, Miss'.

Justin Scroggie for 'There's Something Alive in My Trainers', 'Memory Lane', 'First Lines' and 'The Truth About Henry'.

The Society of Authors as the Literary Representative of the Estate of Alfred Noyes for 'Daddy Fell Into the Pond'.

Kit Wright for 'My Dad, Your Dad', and 'My Party', from *Rabbiting On*.

More Smarties Books

Smarties Books are:

Fun, colourful, interactive, creative, wacky and there's lot's in them.

ONLY SMARTIES HAVE THE ANSWER ®

Smarties Joke Book

By Justin Scroggie
£3.99

Packed full of
rib-tickling,
side-splitting,
stomach-clenching
jokes. It's the
funniest joke
book around.

What do you call a white Smartie?

Why is a classroom like an old car?

How do you count cows?

Why did the jelly roll?

Why is a strawberry like a book?

What do you call an elephant that flies?

Why are fish so smart?

If you want to know the answer to these and
thousands more like them then this is the perfect
book for you. What's more there's crazy cartoons
on every page and there's even a moving picture!

Smarties How To Draw Cartoons
By David Mostyn
£3.99

Everyone can draw wacky cartoons – this shows you how. David Mostyn, a well-known cartoonist and illustrator, has put together this great guide for comic fans everywhere.

There's advice on what material to use, how to get started, how you can stretch a little character into a huge plump one, how to develop action scenes and how to create a whole range of wacky expressions. In fact, all the help you need to bring your drawings to life.

Smarties Smart Science
By Richard Robinson
£3.99

Find out
• what belly buttons are for?
• what happens when your arm goes to sleep?
• what came first, the chicken or the egg?
• why it's colder at the top of a hill, though it's nearer the sun
• how do planes fly?
• how magnifiers magnify

This amazing book reveals the secret science behind some of the most intriguing and mind-blowing questions about the world around us.

Smarties Incredible Facts

By Mike Ashley
£6.99

Did you know that . . . ?
- When you sneeze bits whizz out of your nose as fast as an Intercity train.
- Camels can drink nearly 113 litres of water in half an hour.
- You can sweat enough to fill 126 baths in a year.

YUCK.

Packed full of yucky, funny, naughty, weird and amazing facts about the biggest, the smallest, the longest, the smelliest, the silliest, the fiercest, the dirtiest things.

Smarties Incredible Monsters

Mike Ashley
£6.99

Did you know that . . . ?
- You could park a car on the head of a Torosaurus.
- The bombadier beetle has a bum with a built-in flame-thrower.
- Some people have worms inside them longer than a hosepipe.
- The biggest dinosaur footprints were the size of four dustbin lids.

From deadly dinosaurs to weird deep-sea fish, and from man-eating tigers to tiny but very nasty creepy crawlies. You'll find some facts just plain unbelievable, and some are so strange you'll think we are joking, but we're not . . .

Smarties Puzzle Busters
Justin Scroggie – £2.99
Can you help the puzzle
busters crack exciting
crimes and weird mysteries?

Smarties Chuckle Factory
£2.99
How to giggle your way
through the boring bits of
the holidays.

Smarties Smart Art
Deri Robins – £2.99
For creative geniuses
everywhere, especially on
rainy days.

Smarties Travel Teasers
Justin Scroggie – £2.99
Ridiculous riddles, teasers,
games and puzzles for all those
boring journeys.

How to order

Smarties Books are available from all good bookshops or direct from the publishers.

Just fill in the form below and tick the titles you want over the page.

BS Direct
Colchester Road, Frating Green, Colchester, Essex CO7 7DW
Tel: +44 (0) 1206 255777 Fax: +44 (0) 1206 255914
E-mail: sales@tbs-ltd.co.uk

UK/BFPO customers please allow £1.00 for p&p for the first book, plus 50p for the second, plus 30p for each additional book up to a maximum charge of £3.00.

Please send me the titles ticked.

Overseas customers (inc. Ireland), please allow £2.00 for the first book, plus £1.00 for the second, plus 50p for each additional book.

NAME (Block letters) ....

ADDRESS...

....

POSTCODE ....

I enclose a cheque/PO (payable to TBS Direct) for ....

I wish to pay by Switch/Credit card ....

Number..

Card Expiry Date ....

Switch Issue Number...

Smarties Joke Book ☐
184119 069 1
Price: £3.99

Smarties How to Draw Cartoons ☐
184119 151 5
Price: £3.99

Smarties Smart Science ☐
184119 150 7
Price: £3.99

Smarties Incredible Facts ☐
184119 068 3
Full colour throughout
Price: £6.99

Smarties Incredible Monsters ☐
184119 157 4
Full colour throughout
Price: £6.99

Smarties Travel Teasers ☐
184119 153 5
Price: £2.99

Smarties Smart Art ☐
184119 155 8
Price: £2.99

Smarties Puzzle Busters ☐
Justin Scroggie
184119 154 X
Price: £2.99

The Chuckle Factory ☐
Justin Scroggie
184119 156 6
Price: £2.99